THE ANCIENT EGYPTIANS

JANE SHUTER

HISTORY STARTS HERE!
The Ancient Egyptians
OTHER TITLES IN THE SERIES
The Ancient Greeks • The Ancient Romans
• The Tudors •

Produced for Wayland Publishers Limited by
Roger Coote Publishing
Gissing's Farm
Fressingfield
Suffolk IP21 5SH
England

Designer: Victoria Webb
Editor: Alex Edmonds
Illustrations: Michael Posen
Cover artwork: Kasia Posen

First Published in Great Britain in 1999 by Wayland (Publishers) Ltd
Reprinted in 2003 and 2004 by Hodder Wayland,
an imprint of Hodder Children's Books,
© Hodder Wayland 1999

Hodder Children's Books,
a division of Hodder Headline Limited
338 Euston Road, London NW1 3BH

British Library Cataloguing in Publication Data
Shuter, Jane
  The ancient Egyptians. – (History starts here)
  1.Egypt – Social life and customs – To 332 BC. – Juvenile literature
  2.Egypt – History – To 640 AD. – Juvenile literature
  3.Egypt – Kings and rulers – Juvenile literature
  I.Title
  932
  ISBN 0 7502 4208 6
Printed and bound in China

Front cover picture: Painted limestone statues of Prince Rahotep and
his wife Norfret
Title page picture: Hunting wildfowl in the marshes along the Nile.

Picture acknowledgements:

Ancient Art and Architecture Collection: 5 (R Sheridan),
6 (Mary Jelliffe), 16 (R Sheridan), 12 (R Sheridan), 20 (R Sheridan), 22 (R Sheridan),
24 (R Sheridan), 26 (Mary Jelliffe); CM Dixon: 8, 9, 10, 11, 13, 14, 17, 18, 21, 23, 24-25, 28;
ET Archive: front cover, 1, 19, 27; Tony Stane Images: 29 (Stephen Johnson)

All Wayland books encourage children to
read and help them improve their literacy.

 The contents page, page numbers,
headings and index help locate
specific pieces of information.

 The glossary reinforces alphabetic
knowledge and extends vocabulary.

 The further information section
suggests other books dealing with
the same subject.

CONTENTS

THE FIRST EGYPTIANS

The ancient Egyptians lived by the River Nile, in Egypt. The River Nile flooded each year and the mud it left behind was the only soil that crops could grow on. The rest of Egypt was desert. So people lived close to the river.

Ancient Egypt dates from when Upper and Lower Egypt were first ruled by one pharaoh (king). The green shading shows areas where crops could grow.

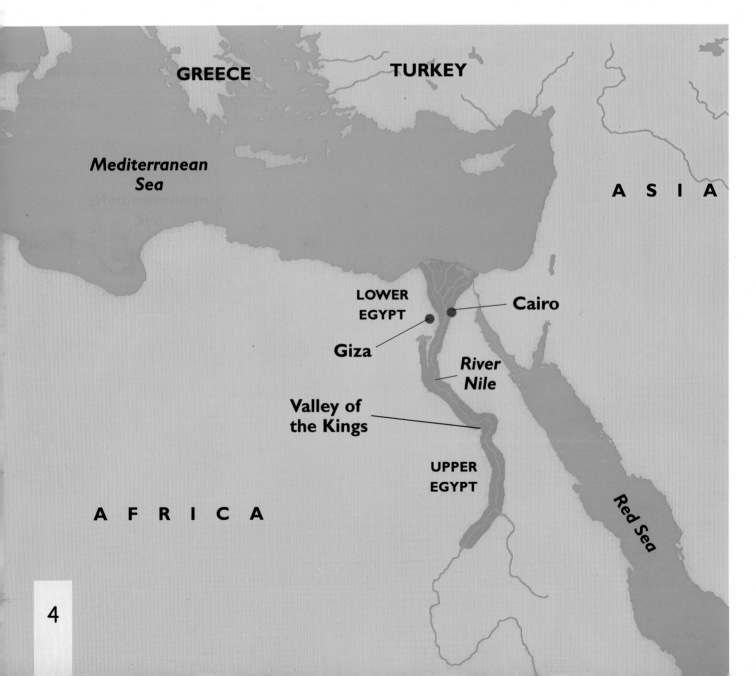

GREECE

TURKEY

Mediterranean Sea

ASIA

LOWER EGYPT

Cairo

Giza

River Nile

Valley of the Kings

UPPER EGYPT

AFRICA

Red Sea

People living in Egypt today still live mostly along the banks of the River Nile. A dam, finished in 1970, was built at Aswan to stop the yearly flooding.

The first ancient Egyptians made their homes along the Nile about 4,000 years ago. They carried on living and working there for about 3,000 years, until other groups of people invaded and took over the country.

RICH AND POOR

A king, the pharaoh, ruled ancient Egypt. He was the most important person in the country and the wealthiest. The least important people were slaves and they were also the poorest people. Everyone else fitted in between.

There were rules about who could do each job. Only a few people moved up into more important jobs. Criminals could lose their jobs. They became slaves, or had to do the hardest, worst paid work.

These prisoners, with their hands tied behind their backs, are shown being taken to Egypt where they will become slaves.

This picture shows the different people in Egyptian society. The most important person, the pharaoh, is at the top, the least important people, slaves, are at the bottom.

PHARAOH

Nobles   **Governors**   **High priests**

Craftworkers   **Scribes**   **Artists**   **Priests and priestesses**

Farmers   **Builders**   **Record-keepers**   **Temple workers**   **Fishermen**

Slaves and criminals

HOUSES AND HOMES

Everyone in ancient Egypt lived in homes built from mudbrick – even the pharaoh. Homes had small windows and air vents in the roof, to keep the heat out. Important people had large, beautifully decorated homes.

The white paint on the outside of this house reflected the heat away from the house.

WHAT'S INSIDE?

Ancient Egyptian houses had white inside walls. Poor people decorated their walls with bands of colour and simple patterns. Rich people had more complicated decorations. Homes had very little furniture. Ordinary houses had a mudbrick shelf instead of beds, one or two chairs and just a few low tables.

Important people had gardens, with pools – cool, shady places to sit in hot weather. Poorer people had small yards or flat roofs where they could relax. They had canopies or climbing plants grown over a frame, for shade.

The trees around the pool in a rich family's garden gave shade and fruit to eat.

FAMILY LIFE

The ancient Egyptians thought family life was very important. A marriage began when a couple set up home together. The most important job for women was having children and running the home, but many women, especially in poorer families, had to work as well.

This wooden model shows a woman making bread. Much of the cooking and food preparation was done on the floor in Egyptian homes.

Here a man sits with his wife and son. Men who owned their own homes were expected to look after other family members.

Women were allowed to own their own homes, but they were not allowed to do some jobs, such as helping to rule the country. Men did all the washing. This was because it was done in the River Nile, which was full of crocodiles.

CHILDREN

The top of this box is a board for a race game. Underneath is a draw to keep the playing pieces safe.

Babies and small children played with balls and dolls, just as they do now. Their parents or, if they came from a rich family, servants played with them and told them stories. But as soon as they could do simple jobs in the home, the workshop or the fields they were expected to work.

CHILDREN'S NAMES

Parents often named their children after a god or goddess. They expected that a child called She Is Named After Mut would be protected by the goddess Mut as she grew up. Other parents gave their children names that showed what they wanted the child to be like such as Happy or Clever.

Wealthy Egyptians wanted their children to be blessed by the gods. Here, Akhenaten and Nefertiti are showing their daughters to the Sun God Aten.

Only boys who were training for jobs where they had to read and write were taught these skills. The rest learned the same trade as their fathers. Some girls, especially in rich families, were taught simple reading and writing at home.

13

CLOTHES

Clothes in ancient Egypt were mostly made from linen. Rich and poor people wore similar clothes, but rich people wore finer cloth, bleached white. Children often wore nothing at all.

Men and women shaved their heads or had very short hair. They wore wigs to dress up. Rich people had wigs made from human hair. Poor people wore wigs made from wool or vegetable fibre. Children's hair was shaved or kept short, except for one long plait at the side, the mark of childhood.

Egyptian men wore jewellery like this pectoral – a big necklace which was worn on the chest. It shows a pharaoh in between two gods.

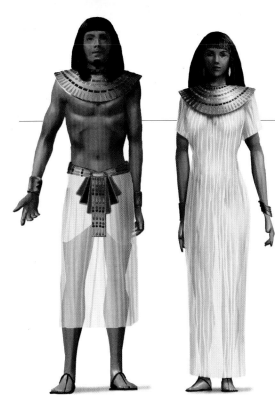

Rich people wore fine clothes, jewellery, make up and wigs much of the time, because they did not need to work.

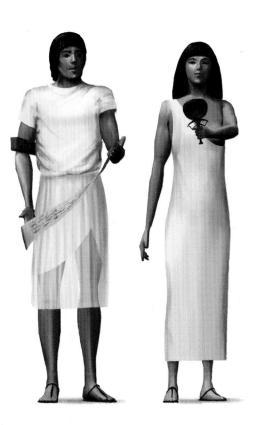

Ordinary people wore clothes made from thicker cloth. They did not wear jewellery while working.

Poor workers needed clothes they could move easily in. The thick linen they used was quite scratchy, but it did not wear out quickly.

FARMING AND TRADE

Every year the River Nile flooded in July. The mud it left behind when it went down in October was the only soil rich enough to grow crops in. So farmers worked hard from November to June, growing enough to feed everyone all year round. While the land was flooded they did other work.

These farmers are going to hit the cut grain to separate it from the stalks (known as threshing).

This wooden model of a grain store has real ancient Egyptian grain in it. Grain was ground into flour by crushing it into powder.

Egyptian workers made paper, jewellery, pottery and cloth. They made sandals and baskets. The ancient Egyptians mostly traded with each other at markets in the towns. They only needed to trade with other countries when their farmers grew too little grain to feed everyone.

FOOD AND DRINK

The most important crop the ancient Egyptians grew was grain. They used grain to make the bread and beer that everyone ate and drank every day. They also ate a lot of vegetables, mostly onions, leeks, cabbage, lettuce and cucumber.

Feasts were a way of marking special occasions, happy or sad. This carving shows a funeral feast.

Poor people did not eat meat very often, or even fish from the river. Rich people ate beef, lamb and goat, ducks and geese as well as all kinds of fish. Owning animals was a sign of how rich a person was. As well as eating farm animals they hunted wild animals for sport and food.

This wall painting shows a rich man, Nebamun, hunting in the marshes with his wife, daughter and specially trained hunting cat.

GODS AND TEMPLES

The ancient Egyptians believed in many different gods and goddesses who controlled everything – from the sun coming up in the morning to crops growing well in the fields. They prayed to their gods at home and in temples, where statues of the gods were kept and cared for.

People wore magic amulets, believing the amulets would keep them safe from danger or illness. These amulets show the eye of the god Horus.

The ancient Egyptians also believed that magic could keep away bad luck or evil spirits, and could help to cure sick people. Doctors often said magic prayers at the same time as they gave a patient medicine.

Ancient Egyptian gods and goddesses were often shown with human bodies and animal heads. Each one had the head of a different animal. This is Anubis, the jackal-headed god.

MUMMIES

The ancient Egyptians believed in life after death. So they preserved the bodies of the dead for when they went to the afterlife. They took out the soft parts that would rot and covered the body in salt to draw out all the fluid. They then wrapped the body in long strips of cloth soaked in oil.

This mummy case is decorated with picture writing, called hieroglyphs.

TOO CLEVER?

Maybe the long, complicated ancient Egyptian mummifying process was too clever. Earlier mummies, buried in hot desert sands which soaked up their body fluids, were preserved just as well!

The soft parts taken out of the body, such as the heart, were preserved in four jars, called canopic jars. Here are two canopic jars.

When the dead had been mummified, they were put into mummy cases made in the shape of a person. They were then buried with food, clothes, make-up and models of things they would need in the afterlife (such as boats).

THE PYRAMIDS

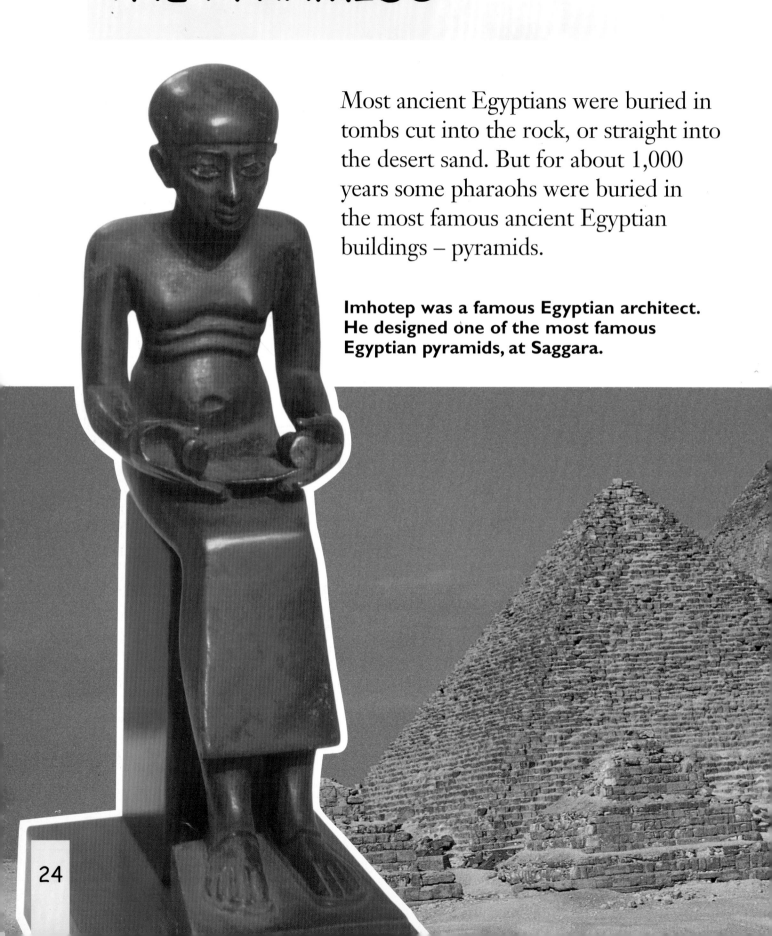

Most ancient Egyptians were buried in tombs cut into the rock, or straight into the desert sand. But for about 1,000 years some pharaohs were buried in the most famous ancient Egyptian buildings – pyramids.

Imhotep was a famous Egyptian architect. He designed one of the most famous Egyptian pyramids, at Saggara.

Pyramids were built from thousands of heavy stone blocks, all cut by hand, pulled on rollers and hauled into place by workmen. It was a long, slow, hard job. The pharaoh's tomb was usually underground, only a few passages and rooms were above ground.

The tallest of the pyramids at Giza was over 146 metres high. It was built from more than 2 million stone blocks.

CHEAT!

The biggest pyramid at Giza is the Great Pyramid, at the back of the picture. It was built by the pharaoh Khufu, who ruled from about 2589 BC to 2566 BC. Khufu's son Kafra had the pyramid in the middle built on higher ground, so it looked as though it was the biggest.

PAINTING AND WRITING

A lot of what we know about the ancient Egyptians comes from studying the beautiful paintings on the walls of their tombs. The paintings usually show people who have died doing ordinary things, such as working, in the afterlife.

Sennedjem and his wife farm in the afterlife, in their best clothes – looking perfect. This is from the wall of his tomb. In real life they would not have farmed at all.

The hieroglyphs around the painting of the artist Maie and his wife tell us about the things that happened in his life.

The ancient Egyptians used two kinds of writing. Hieroglyphs, the complicated picture writing, were used for important papers and writing on the walls of tombs and temples. They used a simplified version of this for everyday writing.

THE END OF ANCIENT EGYPT

This ancient Egyptian water clock measures 24 hours to every day, just as our clocks do.

The ancient Egyptians were very powerful for about 3,000 years. There were times when other countries tried to take over, but these did not last. However in 30 BC Egypt was swallowed up by the Roman Empire. The ancient Egyptian way of life came to an end.

People are still fascinated by the ancient Egyptians. Ordinary people visit Egypt and read books about the ancient Egyptians. Archaeologists are still finding their temples, towns and tombs. Some things that we still use today were invented by the ancient Egyptians. They were the first people to have a year of 365 days divided into 12 months, and they invented clocks.

People still marvel at the Egyptian pyramids and copy the design. This modern glass pyramid is at the Louvre, in Paris.

29

IMPORTANT DATES

All the dates in this list are 'BC' dates. This stands for 'Before Christ'. BC dates are counted back from the year 0, which is the year we say Jesus Christ was born. Some dates have the letter 'c.' in front of them. This stands for 'circa', which means 'about'. These dates are guesses, because nobody knows what the real date is.

c. 12 000 People began to settle down to to live and grow crops along the banks of the River Nile for the first time.

c. 6000 People began to live in bigger groups and farm and keep animals together. They started to make things, like pottery and tools.

c. 3500 People in Lower and Upper Egypt had found out about each other, by sailing up the river. They began to trade things.

c. 3100 Upper and Lower Egypt were joined together under one pharaoh for the first time.

c. 2686–2181 OLD KINGDOM. All of Egypt was ruled by one pharaoh.

c. 3000 From this time on people began to write things down and keep lists and official letters.

c. 2650–2400 The ancient Egyptians built pyramids to bury their pharaohs in.

c. 2181–2055 Egypt was no longer ruled by one pharaoh. Egyptian rulers in different parts of the country often fought each other.

c. 2055–1650 MIDDLE KINGDOM. All of Egypt was ruled by one pharaoh.

c. 2055 The pharaoh Ammenemes I began a system of the pharaoh choosing who would rule after him, and ruling with that person for several years before he died. As the country became more settled, Egypt began trading regularly with other countries. More towns were built along the river, and more temples. Now not only pharaohs were mummified and buried in tombs with belongings, more and more people were buried this way.

c. 1550–1069 NEW KINGDOM. All of Egypt was ruled by one pharaoh.

c. 1550 Pharaohs and other important people were buried in tombs in the rock in the Valley of the Kings and nearby valleys.

c. 1069–747 Egypt was no longer ruled by one pharaoh.

747–30 LATE PERIOD. All of Egypt was ruled by one pharaoh. The Persians then the Greeks ruled Egypt. In 30 BC it was taken over by the Romans.

GLOSSARY

Air vents Holes made in a building that allow air to move around a building and let air into it. Air vents are made to let air in, but not rain, dust or leaves.

Bleached Things are bleached, made white, by soaking them in a weak acid.

Desert Land where little or no rain falls, so the ground is too dry to grow things in.

Family members Everyone who belongs to a family, not just parents and children.

Grain A seed, related to grass, which you can eat.

Mudbrick Building bricks were made from mud that was hardened by drying it in the sun.

Mummify To stop dead bodies from rotting by covering them with special oils.

Linen A cloth made from the stems of the flax plant.

Pharaoh A king of ancient Egypt.

Slaves People who can be bought and sold as if they were possessions, and who have to work for whoever owns them.

Temples Homes for the gods, where priests go to pray to the gods.

Trade To sell or swap something you do not need in return for something you want.

Weavers People who make cloth by weaving threads under and over each other and pushing the threads so close together that you cannot see through.

FURTHER INFORMATION

BOOKS TO READ

Remains to be Seen: Exploring Ancient Egypt by John Malam (Evans Brothers, 2003)

The Search for Tutankamun by Jane Shuter (Heinemann, 1998)

Pharaoh and Embalmer: All in a Day's Work by Anita Ganeri (Heinemann, 1997)

More advanced reading

Ancient Egypt: Food and Farming by Jane Shuter (Heinemann, 1999)

Pyramid by David Macaulay (Houghton Mifflin, 1982)

Family Life in: Ancient Egypt by Peter Clayton (Hodder Wayland, 2001)

INDEX